# foreword

Eggs are loaded with nutrients and vitamins and are an excellent and inexpensive source of protein. They have been lambasted for their cholesterol content, but the much-maligned little gems have been given a bad rap. In truth, eggs can easily fit into a healthy diet.

Perhaps the best thing about eggs, though, is their versatility. Sure, they taste great boiled, fried, scrambled and poached, but they can be used in all types of dishes, both sweet and savoury.

Not only are they a great way to start the morning, they are also excellent at lunch, supper...any time! From frittatas and soups to pastas and desserts, this collection of recipes from the Company's Coming library showcases meals and snacks that will tempt your taste buds any time of the day.

*Jean Paré*

# fruit-full french toast

*This fruit-laden breakfast fare is as pretty as it is tasty. Expect your family or guests to ask for seconds!*

| | | |
|---|---|---|
| Orange marmalade | 1/4 cup | 60 mL |
| Thick whole-wheat bread slices | 6 | 6 |
| Chopped dried apricot | 1/2 cup | 125 mL |
| Dried cranberries | 1/4 cup | 60 mL |
| Large eggs | 4 | 4 |
| Milk | 3/4 cup | 175 mL |
| Applesauce | 1/2 cup | 125 mL |
| Vanilla | 1/2 tsp. | 2 mL |
| Ground cinnamon | 1/2 tsp. | 2 mL |
| Fresh raspberries | 1 cup | 250 mL |
| Fresh blueberries | 1/2 cup | 125 mL |
| Sliced natural almonds, toasted (see Tip, page 64), optional | 2 tbsp. | 30 mL |
| Icing (confectioner's) sugar (optional) | 1 tsp. | 5 mL |

Spread marmalade on 1 side of each bread slice. Cut slices in half diagonally.

Scatter apricot and cranberries in greased 9 x 13 inch (23 x 33 cm) pan. Arrange bread slices, marmalade-side up, in single layer on top of fruit.

Beat eggs and milk with whisk in medium bowl. Add applesauce, vanilla and cinnamon. Stir well. Carefully pour over bread. Cover. Chill overnight. Bake, uncovered, in 450°F (230°C) oven for 20 to 25 minutes until edges are golden.

Scatter raspberries, blueberries and almonds, in order given, over top. Sprinkle with icing sugar. Serves 6.

*1 serving: 302 Calories; 6.3 g Total Fat (2.4 g Mono, 1.1 g Poly, 1.8 g Sat); 145 mg Cholesterol; 54 g Carbohydrate; 7 g Fibre; 12 g Protein; 368 mg Sodium*

# chicken and leek frittata

*If you're looking for a brunch option with some serious class, this is the recipe for you. Try using applewood-smoked Cheddar in this delicious frittata—its distinctive smoky flavour perfectly complements leek and fresh basil.*

| | | |
|---|---|---|
| Cooking oil | 1 tbsp. | 15 mL |
| Boneless, skinless chicken breast halves, chopped | 3/4 lb. | 340 g |
| Thinly sliced leek (white part only) | 1 1/2 cups | 375 mL |
| Large eggs | 10 | 10 |
| Grated smoked Cheddar cheese | 1/2 cup | 125 mL |
| Chopped fresh basil | 3 tbsp. | 45 mL |
| Salt | 1/4 tsp. | 1 mL |
| Pepper | 1/4 tsp. | 1 mL |
| Grated smoked Cheddar cheese | 1/2 cup | 125 mL |

Heat cooking oil in large non-stick frying pan on medium. Add chicken and leek. Cook for about 10 minutes, stirring occasionally, until chicken is no longer pink inside.

Whisk next 5 ingredients in medium bowl. Pour over chicken mixture. Cook, covered, for about 4 minutes until bottom is golden and top is almost set. Remove from heat.

Sprinkle with second amount of cheese. Broil on centre rack in oven for about 4 minutes until top is golden and frittata is set (see Tip, page 64). Let stand for 5 minutes. Cuts into 12 wedges.

*1 wedge:* *148 Calories; 8.9 g Total Fat (3.5 g Mono, 1.2 g Poly, 3.5 g Sat); 181 mg Cholesterol; 2 g Carbohydrate; trace Fibre; 14 g Protein; 176 mg Sodium*

# oven scrambled eggs

*Making scrambled eggs for a crowd? Forget standing at the stove, and let your oven do the work instead. Tomato and green onion add a touch of fresh flavour and bright colour to this simplified breakfast favourite. Instead of plain cream cheese, try using a flavoured variety. Smoked salmon or herb and garlic work particularly well.*

| | | |
|---|---|---|
| Large eggs | 12 | 12 |
| Cream cheese, softened and cut up | 4 oz. | 113 g |
| Milk | 1/2 cup | 125 mL |
| Salt | 1/4 tsp. | 1 mL |
| Pepper | 1/8 tsp. | 0.5 mL |
| Finely chopped tomato | 1/2 cup | 125 mL |
| Finely chopped green onion | 1/4 cup | 60 mL |

Process first 5 ingredients in blender or food processor until smooth. Pour into greased 2 quart (2 L) shallow baking dish. Bake, uncovered, in 375°F (190°C) oven for 15 minutes. Stir. Bake for another 10 to 15 minutes until set.

Sprinkle with tomato and onion. Serves 6.

*1 serving: 224 Calories; 16.7 g Total Fat (6.2 g Mono, 1.7 g Poly, 7.4 g Sat); 394 mg Cholesterol; 3 g Carbohydrate; trace Fibre; 15 g Protein; 286 mg Sodium*

# brunch dish

*A crisp hash brown crust makes this quiche truly unique. Loaded with bacon, green pepper and two kinds of cheese, it is definitely a one-stop brunch dish!*

| | | |
|---|---|---|
| **Bacon slices, diced** | 6 | 6 |
| **Chopped green pepper** | 1/4 cup | 60 mL |
| **Chopped onion** | 1/4 cup | 60 mL |
| **Frozen hash brown potatoes, thawed** | 2 cups | 500 mL |
| **Large eggs** | 4 | 4 |
| **Water** | 1/4 cup | 60 mL |
| **Salt** | 1/2 tsp. | 2 mL |
| **Pepper** | 1/8 tsp. | 0.5 mL |
| **Grated medium Cheddar cheese** | 1/2 cup | 125 mL |
| **Grated part-skim mozzarella cheese** | 1/2 cup | 125 mL |
| **Chopped fresh parsley, for garnish** | | |

Combine first 3 ingredients in large non-stick frying pan on medium. Cook for 5 to 10 minutes, stirring often, until bacon is crisp. Remove with slotted spoon to paper towel to drain. Drain all but 1 tbsp. (15 mL) drippings from pan.

Press hash browns evenly in same frying pan. Cook, uncovered, for about 10 minutes on medium-low, without stirring, until bottom is crisp.

Beat next 4 ingredients in small bowl. Add bacon mixture. Stir. Pour over hash browns.

Sprinkle with Cheddar and mozzarella. Cook, covered, for about 5 minutes, without stirring, until knife inserted in centre comes out clean. Garnish with parsley. Cuts into 4 wedges.

*__1 wedge:__ 289 Calories; 19.5 g Total Fat (7.4 g Mono, 1.8 g Poly, 8.8 g Sat); 224 mg Cholesterol; 10 g Carbohydrate; 1 g Fibre; 19 g Protein; 750 mg Sodium*

# irish breakfast

*A complete breakfast—Irish style! You could use pastrami from the deli or leftover corned beef, if you have any.*

**CORNED BEEF HASH**

| | | |
|---|---|---|
| Butter (or hard margarine) | 1 tbsp. | 15 mL |
| Finely chopped onion | 1/3 cup | 75 mL |
| Finely diced cooked peeled potato | 1 1/2 cups | 375 mL |
| Finely chopped deli corned beef (about 3 1/2 oz., 100 g) | 3/4 cup | 175 mL |
| Pepper | 1/4 tsp. | 1 mL |
| Chopped fresh chives | 2 tsp. | 10 mL |

**POACHED EGGS**

| | | |
|---|---|---|
| White vinegar | 1 tsp. | 5 mL |
| Large eggs | 4 | 4 |
| Chopped fresh chives | 1 tsp. | 5 mL |
| Pepper, sprinkle | | |

**Corned Beef Hash:** Melt butter in medium frying pan on medium. Add onion. Cook for about 3 minutes, stirring occasionally, until onion is starting to brown.

Add potato. Cook for about 5 minutes, stirring occasionally, until potato is golden.

Add corned beef and pepper. Heat and stir for about 1 minute until corned beef is heated through. Add chives. Stir. Remove from heat. Cover to keep warm.

**Poached Eggs:** Pour water into medium saucepan until 1 1/2 inches (3.8 cm) deep. Add vinegar. Stir. Bring to a boil. Reduce heat to medium. Water should continue to simmer. Break 1 egg into shallow dish. Slip egg into water. Repeat with remaining eggs. Cook for 2 to 3 minutes until egg whites are set and yolks reach desired doneness. Transfer eggs with slotted spoon to paper towels to drain. Spoon corned beef mixture onto 2 plates. Top with eggs. Sprinkle with chives and pepper. Serves 2.

*1 serving:* 356 Calories; 16.2 g Total Fat (1.5 g Mono, 0.3 g Poly, 7.5 g Sat); 471 mg Cholesterol; 28 g Carbohydrate; 3 g Fibre; 23 g Protein; 803 mg Sodium

# sunny tuscan eggwiches

*Try the sunny side of Italy! Sun-dried tomato and balsamic vinegar dress up a breakfast classic. To make these into hand-held sandwiches, cook the eggs until fully set and toast 2 additional split English muffins for eggwich tops. The hand-held sandwich variation is easy to eat on the go.*

| | | |
|---|---|---|
| Whole-wheat English muffins, split | 2 | 2 |
| Sun-dried tomato pesto | 1/4 cup | 60 mL |
| Balsamic vinegar | 1 tbsp. | 15 mL |
| Dried crushed chilies | 1/4 tsp. | 1 mL |
| FRIED EGGS | | |
| Olive (or canola) oil | 1 tsp. | 5 mL |
| Large eggs | 4 | 4 |
| Chopped fresh chives | 2 tbsp. | 30 mL |
| Grated Parmesan cheese | 1 tbsp. | 15 mL |

Toast English muffin halves in toaster until golden. Transfer to plate.

Meanwhile, combine next 3 ingredients in a small bowl. Spoon mixture onto muffin halves. Set aside.

**Fried Eggs:** Heat olive oil in a small frying pan on medium. Break eggs into pan. Cook, covered, for about 2 minutes until egg whites are just set and form a light film over yolk.

Carefully place 1 egg over pesto mixture on each muffin half. Sprinkle chives and Parmesan cheese over eggs. Makes 4 eggwiches.

*1 eggwich: 209 Calories; 10.5 g Total Fat (5.3 g Mono, 1.6 g Poly, 2.5 g Sat); 187 mg Cholesterol; 20 g Carbohydrate; 4 g Fibre; 11 g Protein; 363 mg Sodium*

# asian egg thread soup

*Tangy and with just enough heat, this colourful soup is simple to make. For the most visually appealing soup, choose a stir-fry mix that includes baby corn, water chestnuts, carrots and snow peas.*

| | | |
|---|---|---|
| Sesame (or cooking) oil | 1/2 tsp. | 2 mL |
| Sliced fresh brown (or white) mushrooms | 1/2 cup | 125 mL |
| Prepared chicken broth | 2 cups | 500 mL |
| Frozen mixed stir-fry vegetables, larger pieces chopped | 1/2 cup | 125 mL |
| Sliced deli roast pork, julienned, about 1/3 cup (75 mL) | 1 3/4 oz. | 50 g |
| Soy sauce | 1 tbsp. | 15 mL |
| Sweet chili sauce | 1 tbsp. | 15 mL |
| White vinegar | 1 tbsp. | 15 mL |
| Dry sherry (or water) | 1 tbsp. | 15 mL |
| Cornstarch | 1 tbsp. | 15 mL |
| Large egg | 1 | 1 |
| Sliced green onion | 1 tbsp. | 15 mL |

Heat sesame oil in a medium saucepan on medium-high. Add mushrooms. Cook for about 5 minutes, stirring occasionally, until they are softened and starting to brown.

Add next 6 ingredients. Cook for about 5 minutes, stirring occasionally, until boiling and vegetables are tender-crisp.

Stir sherry into cornstarch in a small cup. Stir into soup. Heat and stir until boiling and thickened.

Beat egg with fork in a small cup. Add to soup in thin, steady stream, stirring constantly, until fine threads form.

Sprinkle with green onion. Makes about 2 1/2 cups (625 mL). Serves 2.

*1 serving:* 162 Calories; 6.4 g Total Fat (1.9 g Mono, 1.2 g Poly, 1.7 g Sat); 111 mg Cholesterol; 13 g Carbohydrate; trace Fibre; 10 g Protein; 2316 mg Sodium

# crab asparagus soup

*An egg drop–style soup with sophisticated flavours, this whips up quickly with easy-to-find ingredients.*

| | | |
|---|---|---|
| Cooking oil | 1 tsp. | 5 mL |
| Sliced fresh white mushrooms | 1/2 cup | 125 mL |
| Chopped green onion | 1/4 cup | 60 mL |
| Garlic clove, minced | 1 | 1 |
| Finely grated, peeled ginger root | 1/4 tsp. | 1 mL |
| Pepper | 1/4 tsp. | 1 mL |
| Prepared chicken broth | 3 cups | 750 mL |
| Fresh asparagus, trimmed of tough ends, cut into 1 inch (2.5 cm) pieces | 1/2 lb. | 225 g |
| Can of crabmeat, drained, cartilage removed, flaked | 6 oz. | 170 g |
| Cornstarch | 2 tsp. | 10 mL |
| Soy sauce | 2 tsp. | 10 mL |
| Hoisin sauce | 2 tsp. | 10 mL |
| Large egg | 1 | 1 |
| Water | 1 tbsp. | 15 mL |

Heat cooking oil in a medium saucepan on medium. Add next 5 ingredients. Cook for 5 to 10 minutes, stirring often, until onion is softened.

Add broth. Stir. Bring to a boil on medium-high. Add asparagus and crabmeat. Cover. Reduce heat to medium. Boil gently for about 5 minutes until asparagus is tender-crisp.

Combine next 3 ingredients in a small cup. Add to soup. Heat and stir for about 1 minute until boiling and slightly thickened.

Beat egg and water with fork in same small cup. Add to soup in thin stream, stirring constantly. Makes about 4 1/2 cups (1.1 L).

*1 cup (250 mL): 119 Calories; 3.7 g Total Fat (1.5 g Mono, 0.9 g Poly, 0.8 g Sat); 79 mg Cholesterol; 8 g Carbohydrate; 1 g Fibre; 14 g Protein; 900 mg Sodium*

# hot and sour soup

*This simple soup makes a stimulating start to your meal. A gentle heat and a mild sour tang add to the complex flavours of the broth.*

| | | |
|---|---|---|
| Prepared chicken broth | 6 cups | 1.5 L |
| Boneless pork loin, cut julienne into 1 1/2 inch (3.8 cm) lengths | 7 oz. | 200 g |
| Sliced fresh white mushrooms | 1 cup | 250 mL |
| Water | 1/2 cup | 125 mL |
| Cornstarch | 2 tbsp. | 30 mL |
| White vinegar | 3 tbsp. | 45 mL |
| Soy sauce | 2 tbsp. | 30 mL |
| Chili paste (sambal oelek) | 2 tsp. | 10 mL |
| Pepper | 1/4 tsp. | 1 mL |
| Large egg | 1 | 1 |
| Green onions, sliced | 2 | 2 |

Bring broth to a boil in a large saucepan. Add pork. Return to a boil, then reduce heat. Cover. Boil gently for about 5 minutes until pork is tender.

Add mushrooms. Cover. Simmer for 10 minutes.

Stir water into cornstarch in a small bowl. Add next 4 ingredients. Stir into pork mixture until boiling and slightly thickened.

Beat egg with a fork in a small cup. Add egg to pork mixture in a thin stream, constantly stirring in a circular motion until fine egg threads form. Sprinkle individual servings with green onion. Makes about 7 cups (1.75 L). Serves 6.

*1 serving: 120 Calories; 4.5 g Total Fat (1.9 g Mono, 0.6 g Poly, 1.5 g Sat); 54 mg Cholesterol; 5 g Carbohydrate; trace Fibre; 13 g Protein; 1277 mg Sodium*

# multi-layered salad

*Make this salad the day before, if you like. Just cover it with plastic wrap and chill until ready to serve. It's the perfect salad for company! For a more colourful and nutritious salad, use a mixture of iceberg and romaine lettuce plus some spinach leaves.*

| | | |
|---|---|---|
| Head of iceberg lettuce, chopped or torn | 1 | 1 |
| Sliced celery | 1 cup | 250 mL |
| Large hard-cooked eggs, chopped or sliced | 6 | 6 |
| Cold cooked (or frozen, thawed) peas | 1 cup | 250 mL |
| Chopped green pepper | 1/2 cup | 125 mL |
| Green onions, sliced | 8 | 8 |
| Can of sliced water chestnuts, drained | 8 oz. | 227 mL |
| Bacon slices, cooked crisp and crumbled | 8 | 8 |
| Sour cream | 1 cup | 250 mL |
| Salad dressing (or mayonnaise) | 1 cup | 250 mL |
| Granulated sugar | 2 tbsp. | 30 mL |
| Grated medium Cheddar cheese | 1 cup | 250 mL |
| Bacon slices, cooked crisp and crumbled | 4 | 4 |

Arrange lettuce in bottom of a 3 quart (3 L) glass baking dish or large glass bowl. Layer next 7 ingredients, in order given, on top of lettuce.

Combine sour cream, salad dressing and sugar in a small bowl. Spoon on top of salad. Carefully spread dressing to edge of baking dish to seal. Scatter cheese over dressing. Scatter second amount of bacon over top. Serves 10.

***1 serving:*** *344 Calories; 26.6 g Total Fat (11.9 g Mono, 5.3 g Poly, 7.9 g Sat); 164 mg Cholesterol; 14 g Carbohydrate; 1 g Fibre; 12 g Protein; 431 mg Sodium*

# fettuccine frittata salad

*Green fettuccine noodles combined with soft bites of egg and Asiago cheese. The hot pepper adds a little kick to this creamy dish.*

| | | |
|---|---|---|
| Water | 12 cups | 3 L |
| Salt | 1 1/2 tsp. | 7 mL |
| Spinach fettuccine, broken in half | 8 oz. | 225 g |
| Large eggs, fork-beaten | 3 | 3 |
| Grated Asiago cheese | 1/4 cup | 60 mL |
| Chopped fresh chives | 1 tbsp. | 15 mL |
| Finely diced fresh hot chili pepper (see Tip, page 64) | 1/2 tsp. | 2 mL |
| Salt | 1/4 tsp. | 1 mL |
| Pepper | 1/4 tsp. | 1 mL |
| Cooking oil | 2 tsp. | 10 mL |
| Slivered red pepper | 1 cup | 250 mL |
| Chopped tomato | 3/4 cup | 175 mL |
| Sun-dried tomato dressing | 1/3 cup | 75 mL |
| Chopped fresh basil | 1 tbsp. | 15 mL |

Combine water and salt in a Dutch oven. Bring to a boil. Add pasta. Boil, uncovered, for 11 to 13 minutes, stirring occasionally, until tender but firm. Drain. Rinse with cold water. Drain well. Transfer to a large bowl.

Whisk next 6 ingredients in a small bowl.

Heat cooking oil in a large non-stick frying pan on medium. Pour egg mixture into pan. Reduce heat to medium-low. When starting to set at outside edge, tilt pan and gently lift cooked egg mixture with spatula, easing around pan from outside edge in. Allow uncooked egg mixture to flow onto bottom of pan until egg is softly set. Cook, covered, for about 1 minute until top is set. Transfer to cutting board. Cool. Slice into thin ribbons.

Add remaining 4 ingredients to pasta. Toss. Add egg ribbons. Toss gently. Makes about 5 3/4 cups (1.45 L).

*1 cup (250 mL): 247 Calories; 9.1 g Total Fat (2.1 g Mono, 1.4 g Poly, 2.2 g Sat); 115 mg Cholesterol; 32 g Carbohydrate; 3 g Fibre; 10 g Protein; 357 mg Sodium*

# spanish potato salad

*This attractive, tapas-inspired salad boasts a zesty vegetable medley, with wedges of hard-cooked egg offering a rustic accent. A hearty dish that pairs well with a bold red wine.*

| | | |
|---|---|---|
| Red baby potatoes, quartered | 2 lbs. | 900 g |
| Coarsely chopped onion | 1/2 cup | 125 mL |
| Olive (or cooking) oil | 1 tbsp. | 15 mL |
| Smoked sweet paprika | 1 tsp. | 5 mL |
| Salt | 1/2 tsp. | 2 mL |
| Pepper | 1/4 tsp. | 1 mL |
| Sun-dried tomato dressing | 1/2 cup | 125 mL |
| Smoked sweet paprika | 1/2 tsp. | 2 mL |
| Tomato paste (see Tip, page 64) | 1/2 tsp. | 2 mL |
| Dried crushed chilies | 1/4 tsp. | 1 mL |
| Garlic clove, minced | 1 | 1 |
| Chopped tomato | 2 cups | 500 mL |
| Chopped green pepper | 1 cup | 250 mL |
| Frozen tiny peas, thawed | 1 cup | 250 mL |
| Chopped fresh parsley | 1 tbsp. | 15 mL |
| Large hard-cooked eggs, quartered | 4 | 4 |
| Chopped fresh parsley | 1 tsp. | 5 mL |

Combine first 6 ingredients in a large bowl. Arrange in single layer on greased baking sheet with sides. Bake in 400°F (200°C) oven for about 30 minutes, stirring at halftime, until potato is tender and starting to brown. Return to same large bowl. Let stand until cool.

Combine next 5 ingredients in a small bowl. Add to potato. Add next 4 ingredients. Toss.

Arrange egg wedges around potato mixture. Sprinkle with second amount of parsley. Serves 6.

*1 serving: 283 Calories; 9.6 g Total Fat (3.1 g Mono, 0.9 g Poly, 1.8 g Sat); 141 mg Cholesterol; 39 g Carbohydrate; 5 g Fibre; 10 g Protein; 517 mg Sodium*

# aussie burger salad

*Inspired by Australian burgers, often served with beets and fried egg right in the bun! Lamb and feta patties are served alongside pickled beets, shredded lettuce and herbs for a variety of complementary flavours. If you prefer to barbecue the patties, grill them on greased foil.*

| | | |
|---|---|---|
| Large egg, fork-beaten | 1 | 1 |
| Fine dry bread crumbs | 1/4 cup | 60 mL |
| Chopped fresh mint | 1 tbsp. | 15 mL |
| Dijon mustard | 1 1/2 tsp. | 7 mL |
| Lean ground lamb (or beef) | 1/2 lb. | 225 g |
| Crumbled feta cheese | 1/2 cup | 125 mL |
| | | |
| Cooking oil | 1 tsp. | 5 mL |
| | | |
| Shredded romaine lettuce, lightly packed | 5 cups | 1.25 L |
| Cherry tomatoes, halved | 1 cup | 250 mL |
| Balsamic vinaigrette dressing | 1/3 cup | 75 mL |
| Thinly sliced green onion | 1/4 cup | 60 mL |
| Chopped fresh mint | 1 tbsp. | 15 mL |
| Chopped fresh parsley | 1 tbsp. | 15 mL |
| Bacon slices, cooked crisp and crumbled | 4 | 4 |
| Sliced pickled beets, rinsed and drained | 1 cup | 250 mL |
| Large hard-cooked eggs, quartered | 4 | 4 |

Combine first 4 ingredients in medium bowl. Add lamb and cheese. Mix well. Divide into 12 equal portions. Shape into 2 inch (5 cm) patties.

Heat cooking oil in large frying pan on medium. Add patties. Cook for about 3 minutes per side until browned and internal temperature reaches 160°F (70°C). Transfer to a plate lined with paper towel. Cover to keep warm.

Toss next 7 ingredients in large bowl. Transfer to 4 serving plates. Arrange beets, egg and patties over lettuce mixture. Serves 4.

*1 serving: 423 Calories; 26.0 g Total Fat (4.8 g Mono, 1.6 g Poly, 8.8 g Sat); 326 mg Cholesterol; 20 g Carbohydrate; 3 g Fibre; 27 g Protein; 783 mg Sodium*

# lean chef's salad

*Eat enough of this salad and you'll be a lean chef too! Consider it a full meal deal with plenty of meat, cheese and eggs.*

| | | |
|---|---|---|
| Chopped or torn romaine lettuce, lightly packed | 4 cups | 1 L |
| Green onion, sliced | 1 | 1 |
| Cherry tomatoes, halved | 8 | 8 |
| Fat-free Italian dressing | 1/3 cup | 75 mL |
| Pepper, sprinkle | | |
| Diced light medium Cheddar cheese | 1/2 cup | 125 mL |
| No-fat deli ham slices, cut into thin strips | 3 oz. | 85 g |
| Lean deli smoked turkey breast slices, cut into thin strips | 3 oz. | 85 g |
| Large hard-cooked eggs, chopped | 2 | 2 |
| Fat-free Italian dressing (optional) | 2 tbsp. | 30 mL |

Put first 3 ingredients into large bowl. Drizzle with first amount of dressing. Sprinkle with pepper. Toss well. Arrange on two individual serving plates.

Arrange next 3 ingredients over lettuce mixture. Sprinkle eggs over top. Serve with second amount of dressing on the side. Serves 2.

*1 serving: 328 Calories; 14.9 g Total Fat (2.2 g Mono, 1.0 g Poly, 7.3 g Sat); 277 mg Cholesterol; 16 g Carbohydrate; 3 g Fibre; 36 g Protein; 1878 mg Sodium*

# potato and egg salad

*Tender baby potatoes make this tangy, lemon-flavoured salad extra special.*

| | | |
|---|---|---|
| Red baby potatoes (with peel), larger potatoes halved or quartered | 2 lbs. | 900 g |
| Salt | 1 tsp. | 5 mL |
| Shaved fresh Parmesan cheese | 1/4 cup | 60 mL |
| Finely chopped red onion | 1/4 cup | 60 mL |
| Hard-boiled eggs, cut into 1/3 inch (1 cm) thick slices | 4 | 4 |
| Chopped fresh parsley | 3 tbsp. | 45 mL |
| **LEMON SOUR CREAM DRESSING** | | |
| Olive (or cooking) oil | 3 tbsp. | 50 mL |
| Lemon juice | 1 tbsp. | 15 mL |
| Sour cream | 1 tbsp. | 15 mL |
| Dijon mustard (with whole seeds) | 1 tbsp. | 15 mL |
| Liquid honey | 2 tsp. | 10 mL |
| Garlic clove, minced | 1 | 1 |
| Salt | 1/4 tsp. | 1 mL |
| Pepper, just a pinch | | |

Cook potatoes in water and salt in large saucepan until tender. Drain well. Cool completely. Transfer to large bowl.

Add next 4 ingredients. Toss.

**Lemon Sour Cream Dressing:** Combine all 8 ingredients in jar with tight-fitting lid. Shake well. Drizzle over potato mixture. Toss. Makes 6 cups (1.5 L). Serves 8.

*1 serving: 197 Calories; 9.3 g Total Fat (5.2 g Mono, 1 g Poly, 2.4 g Sat); 111 mg Cholesterol; 22 g Carbohydrate; 2 g Fibre; 7 g Protein; 203 mg Sodium*

# potato cakes benny

*Poached eggs top cheesy mushroom potato patties. Yummy!*

| | | |
|---|---|---|
| Hard margarine (or butter) | 1 tbsp. | 15 mL |
| Chopped fresh white mushrooms | 1 cup | 250 mL |
| Garlic clove, minced | 1 | 1 |
| Mashed potatoes (about 3 medium, uncooked) | 2 cups | 500 mL |
| Large egg, fork-beaten | 1 | 1 |
| Chopped fresh chives | 2 tsp. | 10 mL |
| Pepper | 1/4 tsp. | 1 mL |
| All-purpose flour | 1/4 cup | 60 mL |
| Paprika | 1/4 tsp. | 1 mL |
| Cooking oil | 2 tsp. | 10 mL |
| Grated medium Cheddar cheese | 1 cup | 250 mL |
| White vinegar | 1 tsp. | 5 mL |
| Large eggs | 8 | 8 |

Melt margarine in a small frying pan on medium-high. Add mushrooms and garlic. Cook for 2 to 3 minutes, stirring often, until mushrooms are softened. Transfer to medium bowl.

Add next 4 ingredients. Stir well. Shape mixture into 8 patties, using about 1/4 cup (60 mL) for each.

Combine flour and paprika in small shallow dish. Press both sides of each patty into flour mixture until coated.

Heat cooking oil in large frying pan on medium-high. Add patties. Cook for 1 to 2 minutes per side until golden. Transfer to baking sheet. Sprinkle cheese over each patty. Cover to keep warm.

Poach eggs according to instructions on page 10. Remove each cooked egg with slotted spoon. Place 1 egg on top of each patty. Transfer 2 egg-topped potato cakes to each of 4 plates. Serves 4.

*1 serving:* 477 Calories; 26.7 g Total Fat (10.4 g Mono, 2.9 g Poly, 10.6 g Sat); 516 mg Cholesterol; 34 g Carbohydrate; 2 g Fibre; 25 g Protein; 368 mg Sodium

# pad thai

*This signature dish dazzles. Tender shrimp, fettuccini-style rice noodles and crunchy peanuts are nestled in a tasty sauce—a perfectly balanced interplay of sweetness, spice and tang with a peppery finish.*

| | | |
|---|---|---|
| Medium rice stick noodles | 1/2 lb. | 225 g |
| Brown sugar, packed | 3 tbsp. | 45 mL |
| Fish sauce | 3 tbsp. | 45 mL |
| Lime juice | 3 tbsp. | 45 mL |
| Tamarind liquid (see Tip, page 64) | 3 tbsp. | 45 mL |
| Soy sauce | 2 tbsp. | 30 mL |
| Chili paste (sambal oelek) | 1 tbsp. | 15 mL |
| Pepper | 1/2 tsp. | 2 mL |
| Cooking oil | 3 tbsp. | 45 mL |
| Uncooked extra-large shrimp (peeled and deveined) | 1 lb. | 454 g |
| Sliced green onion | 1/4 cup | 60 mL |
| Garlic cloves, thinly sliced | 3 | 3 |
| Large eggs | 2 | 2 |
| Bean sprouts, trimmed | 2 cups | 500 mL |
| Cilantro leaves | 12 | 12 |
| Unsalted peanuts, coarsely chopped | 1/4 cup | 60 mL |
| Dried crushed chilies | 1/8 tsp. | 0.5 mL |

Cover noodles with warm water and let stand for 30 minutes until softened. Drain well and set aside.

Combine next 7 ingredients and set aside.

Heat a wok or large frying pan on medium-high. Add cooking oil. Add next 3 ingredients and stir-fry for 2 minutes until shrimp just turn pink. Transfer to a plate and cover to keep warm.

Add eggs to wok and break yolks. Cook, without stirring, until partially set. Stir-fry until set. Add bean sprouts, fish sauce mixture and noodles and toss until coated. Add shrimp mixture and stir-fry for 3 minutes until heated through. Transfer to a serving plate.

Sprinkle with remaining 3 ingredients in order given. Makes about 8 cups (2 L).

*1 cup (250 mL):* 309 Calories; 9.9 g Total Fat (4.4 g Mono, 2.7 g Poly, 1.3 g Sat); 140 mg Cholesterol; 38 g Carbohydrate; 2 g Fibre; 18 g Protein; 1048 mg Sodium

# seafood quiche

*A delightful combination of seafood, delicately seasoned with dill. An excellent dish to treat your guests with.*

| | | |
|---|---|---|
| Cooked salad shrimp | 1/2 cup | 125 mL |
| Fresh (or imitation) crabmeat, chopped | 1/2 cup | 125 mL |
| Smoked salmon slices (about 1 oz., 28 g), chopped | 3 | 3 |
| Unbaked 9 inch (22 cm) pie shell | 1 | 1 |
| Grated part-skim mozzarella cheese | 1 cup | 250 mL |
| Large eggs | 3 | 3 |
| Milk | 1 cup | 250 mL |
| Half-and-half cream | 1/2 cup | 125 mL |
| Chopped fresh dill (or 3/4 tsp., 4 mL, dried) | 1 tbsp. | 15 mL |
| Salt | 1/2 tsp. | 2 mL |
| Pepper | 1/8 tsp. | 0.5 mL |
| Cayenne pepper | 1/8 tsp. | 0.5 mL |
| Grated Parmesan cheese | 2 tbsp. | 30 mL |

Scatter first 3 ingredients over bottom of pie shell. Sprinkle with mozzarella cheese.

Whisk next 7 ingredients in medium bowl. Pour over mozzarella cheese.

Sprinkle with Parmesan cheese. Bake on bottom rack in 425°F (220°C) oven for 10 minutes. Reduce heat to 350°F (175°C). Bake for about 50 minutes until set and knife inserted in centre comes out clean. Let stand for 10 minutes. Cuts into 6 wedges.

*1 wedge:* 305 Calories; 15.7 g Total Fat (1.0 g Mono, 0.2 g Poly, 7.2 g Sat); 177 mg Cholesterol; 22 g Carbohydrate; trace Fibre; 18 g Protein; 827 mg Sodium

# bibimbap

*A golden-crisp crust at the bottom is the foundation of this attractive meal.*

| | | |
|---|---|---|
| Korean hot pepper paste | 1/4 cup | 60 mL |
| Brown sugar, packed | 2 tbsp. | 30 mL |
| Sesame oil | 2 tbsp. | 30 mL |
| Soy sauce | 1 tbsp. | 15 mL |
| Garlic cloves, minced | 2 | 2 |
| | | |
| Cooking oil | 1 tbsp. | 15 mL |
| Sesame oil | 1 tbsp. | 15 mL |
| Cooked long-grain rice (about 1 1/3 cup, 325 mL, uncooked) | 4 cups | 1 L |
| | | |
| Cooking oil | 1/2 tsp. | 2 mL |
| Beef rib-eye steak, thinly sliced (see Tip, page 64) | 1/2 lb. | 225 g |
| Korean barbecue sauce | 3 tbsp. | 45 mL |
| Sesame seeds, toasted | 1 tbsp. | 15 mL |
| | | |
| Cooking oil | 1/2 tsp. | 2 mL |
| Enoki mushrooms, stems trimmed | 3 1/2 oz. | 100 g |
| Mirin | 2 tbsp. | 30 mL |
| | | |
| Fresh spinach leaves, lightly packed, blanched and squeezed dry | 3 cups | 750 mL |
| Julienned carrot | 1/2 cup | 125 mL |
| Julienned radish | 1/2 cup | 125 mL |
| Onion sprouts | 1/2 cup | 125 mL |
| | | |
| Cooking oil | 1/2 tsp. | 2 mL |
| Large eggs | 2 | 2 |

Combine first 5 ingredients in a small bowl and set aside.

Heat a cast iron pan on medium. Grease with both oils. Spread rice in bottom and up sides of pan and heat for 20 minutes until bottom is golden and crust has formed. Reduce heat to low.

Heat a wok on medium-high and add cooking oil. Add next 3 ingredients and stir-fry for 3 minutes until browned. Arrange in a wedge over the rice.

Wipe wok clean and heat cooking oil on medium-high. Add mushrooms and mirin and stir-fry for 1 minute until softened. Arrange in a smaller wedge next to meat mixture.

Arrange next 4 ingredients in wedges over remaining rice.

Fry eggs in wok (see page 12). Place in centre of dish. Toss in pan before serving. Serve with pepper sauce. Serves 4.

*1 serving:* 1152 Calories; 24.6 g Total Fat (4.7 g Mono, 2.4 g Poly, 4.3 g Sat); 138 mg Cholesterol; 193 g Carbohydrate; 8 g Fibre; 36 g Protein; 1381 mg Sodium

# egg foo yong

*Each bite of these omelets contains an excellent combination of flavours and textures. They can be served with the complementary sauce or on their own.*

| | | |
|---|---|---|
| Large eggs | 6 | 6 |
| Salt | 1/2 tsp. | 2 mL |
| Cooking oil | 1 tbsp. | 15 mL |
| Pork tenderloin, trimmed of fat and cut into strips | 8 oz. | 225 g |
| Fresh bean sprouts (about 3 cups, 750 mL), chopped once or twice | 8 oz. | 225 g |
| Thinly sliced celery | 1/3 cup | 75 mL |
| Sliced green onion | 1/3 cup | 75 mL |
| Light-coloured (or regular) soy sauce | 1 tbsp. | 15 mL |
| Cooking oil | 1 tbsp. | 15 mL |
| SAUCE | | |
| Prepared chicken broth | 1 cup | 250 mL |
| Oyster sauce | 1 tbsp. | 15 mL |
| Cornstarch | 1 tbsp. | 15 mL |
| Fancy (mild) molasses | 1 tbsp. | 15 mL |

Beat eggs and salt with fork in large bowl. Set aside.

Heat large non-stick frying pan on medium-high. Add first amount of cooking oil. Add pork. Stir-fry for 1 minute. Add bean sprouts, celery and onion. Stir-fry for 2 to 3 minutes until slightly softened. Add soy sauce. Cover. Cook for 3 minutes. Remove cover. Add to egg mixture. Stir.

Add 1/2 tsp. (2 mL) of second amount of cooking oil to hot frying pan. Add about 1/3 cup (75 mL) egg mixture for each omelet. Cook on medium for about 2 minutes, turning at halftime, until set and lightly browned. Remove to serving platter. Keep warm. Repeat with remaining cooking oil and egg mixture.

**Sauce:** Combine all 4 ingredients in small saucepan. Heat and stir on medium for 5 to 10 minutes until boiling and thickened. Serve over Egg Foo Yong. Serves 4.

*1 serving: 277 Calories; 16.1 g Total Fat (8.1 g Mono, 3.4 g Poly, 3.4 g Sat); 312 mg Cholesterol; 7 g Carbohydrate; trace Fibre; 24 g Protein; 807 mg Sodium*

# fettuccine carbonara

*A delightful, creamy sauce coats these long, flat noodles. The bacon and the savoury flavour of the Parmesan cheese go very well together. Serve with a green salad and sliced ripe tomatoes.*

| | | |
|---|---|---|
| Package of fettuccine | 8 3/4 oz. | 250 g |
| Boiling water | 8 cups | 2 L |
| Salt | 1 tsp. | 5 mL |
| Bacon slices, chopped | 8 | 8 |
| Whipping cream | 1 cup | 250 mL |
| Large eggs, fork-beaten | 3 | 3 |
| Finely grated fresh Parmesan cheese | 1 cup | 250 mL |
| Salt | 1/4 tsp. | 1 mL |
| Pepper, sprinkle | | |

Cook fettuccine in boiling water and first amount of salt in large uncovered pot or Dutch oven for about 10 minutes until tender but firm. Drain well. Return to pot.

Cook bacon in medium frying pan on medium-high for about 5 minutes until crisp. Drain. Add whipping cream. Heat and stir for 2 to 3 minutes. Add to fettuccine. Stir. Add egg and cheese. Stir until combined. Add second amount of salt and pepper. Stir. Makes 4 cups (1 L).

*1 cup (250 mL): 683 Calories; 36.7 g Total Fat (11.8 g Mono, 2.1 g Poly, 20.3 g Sat); 260 mg Cholesterol; 51 g Carbohydrate; 2 g Fibre; 36 g Protein; 2005 mg Sodium*

# huevos rancheros casserole

*A hearty, satisfying Mexican-style casserole that the whole family is sure to love! Loaded with eggs, corn and beans, all topped with a refreshing burst of colour from avocado and tomato.*

| | | |
|---|---|---|
| Can of black beans, rinsed and drained | 19 oz. | 540 mL |
| Fresh (or frozen, thawed) kernel corn | 1 cup | 250 mL |
| Salsa | 1 cup | 250 mL |
| Large eggs | 10 | 10 |
| Finely chopped green onion | 2 tbsp. | 30 mL |
| Milk | 2 tbsp. | 30 mL |
| Salt | 1/8 tsp. | 0.5 mL |
| Grated medium Cheddar cheese | 1 cup | 250 mL |
| Chopped avocado | 1/2 cup | 125 mL |
| Chopped tomato | 1/2 cup | 125 mL |
| Crushed tortilla chips | 1/4 cup | 60 mL |
| Chopped fresh cilantro (or parsley) | 2 tsp. | 10 mL |

Combine first 3 ingredients in greased shallow 2 quart (2 L) casserole.

Whisk next 4 ingredients in medium bowl. Pour over black bean mixture. Sprinkle with cheese. Bake, uncovered, in 350°F (175°C) oven for about 50 minutes until set and golden.

Scatter remaining 4 ingredients, in order given, over top. Serve immediately. Serves 8.

*1 serving:* 250 Calories; 12.0 g Total Fat (3.5 g Mono, 1.0 g Poly, 4.5 g Sat); 185 mg Cholesterol; 23 g Carbohydrate; 6 g Fibre; 15 g Protein; 530 mg Sodium

# special ham fried rice

*You'll be especially pleased at how quickly you can whip up this quick and easy treat. We don't call it special for nothing!*

| | | |
|---|---|---|
| Cooking oil | 1 tbsp. | 15 mL |
| Chopped onion | 2/3 cup | 150 mL |
| Chopped celery | 2/3 cup | 150 mL |
| Cooking oil | 1 tbsp. | 15 mL |
| Large eggs | 2 | 2 |
| Pepper | 1/8 tsp. | 0.5 mL |
| Cold cooked long grain white rice (about 1 cup, 250 mL, uncooked) | 3 cups | 750 mL |
| Chopped cooked ham (about 6 oz., 170 g) | 1 cup | 250 mL |
| Soy sauce | 2 tbsp. | 30 mL |
| Frozen peas, thawed | 1/2 cup | 125 mL |
| Green onions, sliced | 2 | 2 |

Heat wok or large frying pan on medium-high until very hot. Add first amount of cooking oil. Add onion and celery. Stir-fry for about 3 minutes until tender-crisp. Transfer to small bowl. Cover to keep warm.

Add second amount of cooking oil to hot wok. Add eggs and pepper. Break yolks but do not scramble. Cook, without stirring, for 1 minute. Turn. Chop egg with edge of pancake lifter until egg is in small pieces and starting to brown.

Add next 3 ingredients. Stir-fry for about 2 minutes, breaking up rice, until dry and starting to brown. Add onion mixture, peas and green onion. Stir-fry for about 1 minute until heated through. Serves 4.

*1 serving:* *334 Calories; 11.9 g Total Fat (6.2 g Mono, 2.8 g Poly, 2.1 g Sat); 115 mg Cholesterol; 41 g Carbohydrate; 2 g Fibre; 15 g Protein; 1170 mg Sodium*

# macaroons

*The perfect macaroon—sweet and chewy in the middle, crispy on the outside. Drizzle these with melted chocolate for an extra-special treat.*

| | | |
|---|---|---|
| Granulated sugar | 3/4 cup | 175 mL |
| Cornstarch | 2 tbsp. | 30 mL |
| Salt | 1/8 tsp. | 0.5 mL |
| Egg whites (large) | 3 | 3 |
| Shredded (long thread) coconut | 4 cups | 1 L |

Combine sugar, cornstarch and salt in small bowl.

Beat egg whites on high in top of double boiler or large heatproof bowl for about 5 minutes until stiff, dry peaks form. Place over boiling water in double boiler or medium saucepan. Add sugar mixture in 3 additions, beating on medium-high for about 1 minute until smooth and glossy. Cook for about 6 minutes, without stirring, until dry crust forms around edge.

Fold meringue into coconut in large bowl until well combined. Drop, using 2 tsp. (10 mL) for each, about 2 inches (5 cm) apart onto greased cookie sheets. Bake in 350°F (175°C) oven for about 12 minutes until golden. Let stand on cookie sheets for 5 minutes before removing to wire racks to cool. Makes about 48 macaroons.

***1 macaroon:*** *67 Calories; 5.1 g Total Fat (0.2 g Mono, 0.1 g Poly, 4.5 g Sat); 0 mg Cholesterol; 6 g Carbohydrate; trace Fibre; 1 g Protein; 13 mg Sodium*

# cappuccino stack

*These light, tasty morsels are a perfect mid-afternoon snack.*

| | | |
|---|---|---|
| Icing (confectioner's) sugar | 2 tbsp. | 30 mL |
| Instant coffee granules, crushed to a fine powder | 2 tsp. | 10 mL |
| Cornstarch | 1 1/2 tsp. | 7 mL |
| Skim milk powder | 1 1/2 tsp. | 7 mL |
| Ground cinnamon, pinch | | |
| Egg whites (large), room temperature | 2 | 2 |
| Brown sugar, packed | 2 tbsp. | 30 mL |
| Vanilla extract | 1/2 tsp. | 2 mL |
| Semi-sweet chocolate baking square (1 oz., 28 g), chopped | 1 | 1 |

Combine first 5 ingredients.

Beat egg whites until soft peaks form. Gradually add brown sugar, beating until stiff peaks form. Fold in vanilla and coffee mixture. Spoon into a large freezer bag with a corner snipped off. Pipe in a spiral pattern onto a baking sheet lined with parchment paper, leaving a 1/2 inch (12 mm) space between each round. Bake in a 250°F (120°C) oven for 1 1/2 hours. Let stand on baking sheet set on a wire rack until cool. Break into pieces and stack on a large plate.

Microwave chocolate on medium (50%) for about 1 minute, stirring every 15 seconds, until almost melted. Stir until smooth. Drizzle over meringue stack. Serves 6.

*1 serving: 62 Calories; 1.3 g Total Fat (0 g Mono, 0 g Poly, 0.8 g Sat); trace Cholesterol; 11 g Carbohydrate; trace Fibre; 2 g Protein; 23 mg Sodium*

# coffee meringues

*These fancy little meringues are perfect with your after-dinner coffee.*
*Elegantly dipped in chocolate.*

| | | |
|---|---|---|
| Egg whites (large), room temperature | 2 | 2 |
| Cream of tartar | 1/2 tsp. | 2 mL |
| Granulated sugar | 1/3 cup | 75 mL |
| Icing (confectioner's) sugar | 1/3 cup | 75 mL |
| Instant coffee granules | 1 tbsp. | 15 mL |
| Warm water | 1 tbsp. | 15 mL |
| Semi-sweet chocolate baking squares (1 oz., 28 g, each), chopped | 4 | 4 |

Beat egg whites and cream of tartar in medium bowl on medium until soft peaks form. Add granulated sugar 1 tbsp. (15 mL) at a time, beating constantly until stiff peaks form and sugar is dissolved. Fold in icing sugar.

Stir coffee granules into warm water in small cup until dissolved. Fold into meringue. Spoon meringue into piping bag fitted with large plain tip. Pipe 1 inch (2.5 cm) diameter mounds, lifting tip to create pointed end on each, about 2 inches (5 cm) apart onto cookie sheets lined with parchment paper. Bake on bottom rack in 225°F (110°C) oven for 35 to 40 minutes until dry. Turn oven off. Let stand in oven until cooled completely.

Heat chocolate in small heavy saucepan on lowest heat, stirring often until almost melted. Do not overheat. Remove from heat. Stir until smooth. Transfer to small custard cup. Dip each meringue halfway into chocolate, allowing excess to drip back into cup. Place on same parchment paper-lined cookie sheets. Let stand until set. Do not chill. Makes about 48 meringues.

*1 meringue: 21 Calories; 0.7 g Total Fat (0.2 g Mono, 0 g Poly, 0.4 g Sat); 0 mg Cholesterol; 4 g Carbohydrate; trace Fibre; 0 g Protein; 3 mg Sodium*

# orange swirls

*This citrusy, light dessert is totally refreshing.*

**MERINGUES**

| | | |
|---|---|---|
| Egg whites (large), room temperature | 3 | 3 |
| Cream of tartar | 1/4 tsp. | 1 mL |
| Granulated sugar | 1/2 cup | 125 mL |
| Icing (confectioner's) sugar, sifted | 1/2 cup | 125 mL |

**FILLING**

| | | |
|---|---|---|
| Egg yolks (large) | 3 | 3 |
| Orange juice | 1/4 cup | 60 mL |
| Frozen concentrated orange juice | 3 tbsp. | 45 mL |
| Granulated sugar | 3 tbsp. | 45 mL |
| Grated orange zest | 2 tsp. | 10 mL |
| Whipping cream (or 1 envelope of dessert topping, prepared) | 1 cup | 250 mL |
| Orange segments | | |

**Meringues:** Line bottom of 11 x 17 inch (28 x 43 cm) baking sheet with parchment (not waxed) paper. Trace six 3 inch (7.5 cm) circles about 2 inches (5 cm) apart on paper. Turn paper over. Beat egg whites and cream of tartar in large bowl until soft peaks form. Add granulated sugar, 1 tbsp. (15 mL) at a time, beating constantly until stiff peaks form and sugar is dissolved. Fold icing sugar into egg white mixture. Spoon into piping bag fitted with small open star tip. Pipe onto circles, filling each circle completely. Pipe meringue around edge of each circle twice to make sides. Bake in 200°F (95°C) oven for about 1 hour until dry. Turn oven off. Let stand in oven until cool.

**Filling:** Combine first 4 ingredients in top of double boiler or heatproof bowl set over simmering water. Cook, stirring constantly with whisk, until thickened. Remove from heat. Add orange zest. Stir. Cover with plastic wrap directly on surface to prevent skin from forming. Chill until cooled completely.

Beat whipping cream until soft peaks form. Fold into orange mixture until no white streaks remain. Spoon into meringues. Chill for 1 hour. Garnish with orange segments. Serves 6.

*1 serving:* *311 Calories; 16.5 g Total Fat (5.1 g Mono, 0.9 g Poly, 9.4 g Sat); 146 mg Cholesterol; 38 g Carbohydrate; trace Fibre; 4 g Protein; 46 mg Sodium*

# jackfruit mousse

*This smooth, pale yellow mousse balances a light frothiness with the appealing texture of jackfruit. It can be made up to two days in advance.*

| | | |
|---|---|---|
| Can of jackfruit (with syrup) | 20 oz. | 565 mL |
| Granulated sugar | 1/4 cup | 60 mL |
| Unflavoured gelatin | 2 tsp. | 10 mL |
| Egg yolks (large) | 4 | 4 |
| Granulated sugar | 1/4 cup | 60 mL |
| Lemon juice | 1 tbsp. | 15 mL |
| Water | 1 tbsp. | 15 mL |
| Whipped cream | 1 cup | 250 mL |

Process jackfruit and sugar in blender or food processor until smooth and pour into saucepan. Sprinkle gelatin over jackfruit mixture and let stand for 1 minute. Heat and stir on medium until gelatin is dissolved. Set aside.

Whisk next 4 ingredients in a medium stainless steel bowl. Set over simmering water in a large saucepan so that bottom of bowl is not touching water. Whisk for 15 minutes until mixture is thickened and doubled in volume. Remove from heat and fold in jackfruit mixture. Chill for 2 hours, stirring once or twice, until almost set.

Fold in whipped cream. Spoon or pipe into 6 glasses or bowls and chill for 4 hours or overnight. Serves 6.

*1 serving:* 315 Calories; 17.6 g Total Fat (5.5 g Mono, 1.0 g Poly, 10.2 g Sat); 191 mg Cholesterol; 36 g Carbohydrate; 1 g Fibre; 3 g Protein; 29 mg Sodium

# strawberry and papaya with lemon grass sabayon

*Vivid fresh fruit automatically attracts attention—but pour a sweet, creamy sabayon infused with lemon grass over top and the result really turns heads.*

| | | |
|---|---|---|
| Egg yolks (large) | 4 | 4 |
| Dry sherry | 2 tbsp. | 30 mL |
| Granulated sugar | 2 tbsp. | 30 mL |
| Lemon grass paste | 4 tsp. | 20 mL |
| Lemon juice | 1 tsp. | 5 mL |
| Sliced papaya | 1 1/2 cups | 375 mL |
| Sliced fresh strawberries | 1 1/2 cups | 375 mL |

Whisk first 5 ingredients in a medium stainless steel bowl. Set over simmering water in a large saucepan so that bottom of bowl is not touching water. Whisk for 5 minutes until mixture is foamy and thickened enough to leave a path on the back of a spoon when you run your finger over it.

Arrange fruit on 6 serving plates. Drizzle with sabayon. Serves 6.

*1 serving:* 90 Calories; 3.5 g Total Fat (1.3 g Mono, 0.5 g Poly, 1.1 g Sat); 137 mg Cholesterol; 12 g Carbohydrate; 1 g Fibre; 2 g Protein; 78 mg Sodium

# pineapple glory pie

*Maraschino cherries give this glorious pie its pink colour. A lush, juicy treat with an excellent shortbread crust.*

| | | |
|---|---|---|
| All-purpose flour | 1 1/2 cups | 375 mL |
| Granulated sugar | 2 tbsp. | 30 mL |
| Butter (or hard margarine) | 3/4 cup | 175 mL |
| Can of crushed pineapple (with juice) | 19 oz. | 540 mL |
| Granulated sugar | 2/3 cup | 150 mL |
| Cornstarch | 3 tbsp. | 45 mL |
| Lemon juice | 1 tsp. | 5 mL |
| Chopped maraschino cherries | 1/3 cup | 75 mL |
| Maraschino cherry juice | 3 tbsp. | 45 mL |
| Almond extract | 1 tsp. | 5 mL |
| Egg whites (large), room temperature | 3 | 3 |
| Cream of tartar | 1/4 tsp. | 1 mL |
| Granulated sugar | 1/4 cup | 60 mL |
| Vanilla extract | 1 tsp. | 5 mL |
| Medium unsweetened coconut | 2 tbsp. | 30 mL |

Combine flour and sugar in medium bowl. Cut in butter until mixture resembles coarse crumbs. Press firmly in bottom and up side of 9 inch (23 cm) pie plate. Bake in 350°F (175°C) oven for about 15 minutes until

For filling, stir next 4 ingredients in small saucepan until cornstarch is dissolved. Heat and stir on medium until boiling and thickened. Remove from heat. Stir in next 3 ingredients. Pour into crust.

For meringue, beat egg whites and cream of tartar until soft peaks form. Add sugar, 1 tbsp. (15 mL) at a time, beating constantly until stiff peaks form and sugar is dissolved. Add vanilla. Stir. Spoon over filling. Spread evenly to edge of pastry. Sprinkle with coconut. Bake in 350°F (175°C) oven for 10 to 12 minutes until golden. Cool. Cuts into 8 wedges.

*1 wedge:* 409 Calories; 17.8 g Total Fat (4.5 g Mono, 0.7 g Poly, 11.5 g Sat); 45 mg Cholesterol; 59 g Carbohydrate; 2 g Fibre; 4 g Protein; 149 mg Sodium

# recipe index

# topical tips

**Chopping hot peppers:** Hot peppers contain capsaicin in the seeds and ribs. Remove the seeds and ribs to reduce the heat. Wear gloves when handling hot peppers, and do not touch your face near your eyes.

**How to make tamarind liquid:** Place 1/4 cup (60 mL) chopped tamarind pulp into a small bowl. Pour 3/4 cup (175 mL) boiling water over the pulp. Stir to break up the pulp and let stand for 5 minutes. Press through a fine sieve and discard solids. Makes 1/2 cup (125 mL).

**Non-ovenproof pans:** When baking or broiling food in a frying pan with a non-ovenproof handle, wrap the handle in foil and keep it to the front of the oven, away from the element.

**Slicing meat:** Partially freezing the meat before slicing makes it easier to get attractive, evenly thin slices.

**Toasting nuts:** To toast nuts, seeds or coconut, spread evenly in ungreased shallow pan. Bake in 350°F (175°C) oven for 5 to 10 minutes, stirring or shaking often, until desired doneness.

**Tomato paste:** If a recipe calls for less than an entire can of tomato paste, freeze the unopened can for 30 minutes. Open both ends and push the contents through one end. Slice off only what you need. Freeze the remaining paste in a resealable freezer bag or plastic wrap for future use.

## Nutrition Information Guidelines

Each recipe is analyzed using the Canadian Nutrient File from Health Canada, which is based on the United States Department of Agriculture (USDA) Nutrient Database.

- If more than one ingredient is listed (such as "butter or hard margarine"), or if a range is given (1 – 2 tsp., 5 – 10 mL), only the first ingredient or first amount is analyzed.

- For meat, poultry and fish, the serving size per person is based on the recommended 4 oz. (113 g) uncooked weight (without bone), which is 2 – 3 oz. (57 – 85 g) cooked weight (without bone)— approximately the size of a deck of playing cards.

- Milk used is 1% M.F. (milk fat), unless otherwise stated.

- Cooking oil used is canola oil, unless otherwise stated.

- Ingredients indicating "sprinkle," "optional" or "for garnish" are not included in the nutrition information.

- The fat in recipes and combination foods can vary greatly depending on the sources and types of fats used in each specific ingredient. For these reasons, the count of saturated, monounsaturated and polyunsaturated fats may not add up to the total fat content.